TATTING BUTTERFLIES

Teri Dusenbury

DOVER PUBLICATIONS, INC.
Mineola, New York

Dedicated to Kyle Keeton Dusenbury and Oliver Harvey Dusenbury for their encouragement, inspiration, and love.

Copyright

Copyright © 1990, 1992, 1993, 1994, 1997 by Teri Dusenbury.
All rights reserved under Pan American and International Copyright Conventions.

Published in Canada by General Publishing Company, Ltd., 30 Lesmill Road, Don Mills, Toronto, Ontario.
Published in the United Kingdom by Constable and Company, Ltd., 3 The Lanchesters, 162-164 Fulham Palace Road, London W6 9ER.

Bibliographical Note

Tatting Butterflies, first published by Dover Publications, Inc., in 1997, is a revised, corrected, and completely reset publication of patterns from *TATtle TALES 1994*, 1994; *Papillon, Schmetterling, Vlinders, Lepidoptera, Butterflies*, 1994 (both originally published by Teri Dusenbury, Port Orchard, Washington), and various issues of *TATtle TALES* (originally published by Teri Dusenbury, Port Orchard, Washington).

Library of Congress Cataloging-in-Publication Data

Dusenbury, Teri.
    Tatting butterflies / Teri Dusenbury.
        p. cm.
    Combined reprint of two works originally published by the author in 1994 as Tattle tales and as Papillon, Schmetterling, vlinders, Lepidoptera, butterflies.
    Includes bibliographical references.
    ISBN 0-486-29665-2 (pbk.)
    1. Tatting—Patterns. 2. Butterflies in art. I. Dusenbury, Teri. Tattle tales. II. Dusenbury, Teri. Papillon, Schmetterling, vlinders, Lepidoptera, butterflies. III. Title.
TT840.T38D85 1997
746.43'6—dc21   97-22707
                                                                           CIP

Manufactured in the United States of America
Dover Publications, Inc., 31 East 2nd Street, Mineola, N. Y. 11501

Introduction

I love butterflies! The first tatting I ever saw was a butterfly motif. That's all it took—I was immediately hooked! I yearned to be able to tat butterflies, but first I needed to learn how to tat. I tried teaching myself to manipulate the shuttle (traditional style) from a magazine article, but to no avail. I just couldn't figure out how to transfer the hitches that comprised the main knot. My only hope was to find a teacher who could show me the secret behind the sliding double knot.

Unfortunately, it was several years before I learned to tat. I had been living abroad for a number of years, and it wasn't until I returned home to Washington state that my desire to tat was rekindled. After reading Mary Sue Kuhn's book, *The Joy of Tatting*, I again tried in vain to teach myself how to manipulate the shuttle in the traditional style. It was definitely time to find a teacher.

If it weren't for my neighbor Glenda Reed's interest in ceramics, I would never have entered this particular store, nor seen the tatted bookmarks in the display case and inquired if a teacher was available. I'm not sure if it was fate or sheer luck, but I had finally found a teacher and, at long last, was going to learn to tat.

Nani Diaz was the perfect patient teacher. An immigrant from Spain, Nani taught tatting using "original" techniques now referred to as the Riego style. (Mlle. Eleonore Riego de la Branchardière manipulated the sequence of her knots just as one would while tatting directional rings. The only difference was that there was no reversing of the lace to the back side, nor was the shuttle brought through the ring to the front side before closing the ring.) Two hours was all the time I needed to learn the skill required to transfer the hitches. I was tatting!

It wasn't until after I sold my first tatting pattern that I realized from Rebecca Jones' book, *The Complete Book of Tatting*, that I was manipulating my shuttle and knots in true Riego style.

It was easy to teach myself the Reverse Riego style of shuttle manipulation from Ms. Jones' book. After all, I already had the skill required to transfer the hitches from one thread to another. I only needed to reverse the order of hitches to complete a right-sided double knot.

Originally, tatted lace had no front or back side. Today, traditionalists determine the front and back side by whether there is a majority of rings or chains in the design. I don't like the look of the split hitches that appear in traditional tatting. I prefer the appearance of tatted lace where all of the bars of all the knots face one side—the front. Once you become accustomed to my modern techniques, you will appreciate the uniform look your lace will have. These modern tatting techniques contribute to the natural progression this art form is taking in its evolution.

I eventually learned the traditional style of shuttle manipulation, but not from a book. Susan Ackerman Diermyer, the pioneer of tatting videos, sent me her video, *Tat the Easy Way*. Watching Susan's demonstrations, I was able to manipulate my shuttle using the traditional style. The traditional style of shuttle manipulation is an advanced form of tatting and is, therefore, just another manipulation option for the experienced tatter. It is *not* the appropriate style of shuttle manipulation to teach an individual who just wants to learn the basics of tatting.

Tatting is not defined by the implement used to carry the excess thread, nor is it about how "fast" an individual can maneuver that implement. Tatting is defined by the transference of the hitches that comprise the knot from one thread to another, resulting in the end product—tatted lace.

If you teach tatting, try teaching your next student using the Reverse Riego style of shuttle manipulation and see how quickly they learn to transfer the knot.

If you just want to learn the basics of modern tatting, this book is an excellent primer. If you're a novice tatter (meaning you have already learned to transfer the knot and can tat a ring), this is the perfect next step. If you're an experienced traditional tatter, it's never too late to learn new tricks. These techniques, once mastered, can give the traditional tatter the skills to tat any pattern using modern principles.

The Novice Butterfly is my favorite butterfly motif. Variations of this motif have appeared throughout my designs. Start with this motif if you're a novice, or just want to "warm-up" to consistent knotting before attempting to tat any of the first five butterfly designs. You will learn a new join technique and how to join the last ring to the first ring from tatting this pattern.

Butterflies 1–5 are all related to each other in terms of design. Whenever I design butterflies, I can always see another one emerging before completing the first. Because these butterflies are similar in design, it is easy to go from one to another, learning these modern tatting techniques along the way. Tat the first five butterflies and then you'll be ready to tat the variations from the schematic drawings alone. Once you've tatted them all you might see variations of your own waiting to be tatted. You will learn a new join technique, mock rings, directional rings, joining with lock knots, and beading from tatting these butterflies and their variations.

Last, but not least, is the "Tatbit in Flight Charmer Chatelaine." The motif "Tatbit" is being carried off by butterflies to a tatting paradise. Tatbit can hold a crochet hook and be used as a chatelaine, or can hold your favorite charm or a locket with a picture of a loved one inside. If you would like to include stacked butterflies on your Charmer Chatelaine, the directions are included in the techniques section. Tat just the Tatbit motif being carried off by one butterfly motif for earrings or for a pin. Split rings, the lark's head knot chain or reverse double knot chain, the Dora Young Knot, and stacking are the skills you will learn from tatting this pattern or variations of it.

I've incorporated the tatting genius of the late Dora Young into the Tatbit motif. Instead of joining the arms and legs with lock knots, I've used the Dora Young Knot. Ms. Young devised a remarkable knotting technique that enables the tatter to tat a double knot on a fixed thread without taking the thread off the shuttle.

Ms. Young also invented split chain tatting (sometimes referred to as "bridging") using this brilliant technique. Once you've learned the Dora Young Knot, you can substitute this knot for the center lock knots in each of the butterflies for a slightly different look.

I'm also using a new basic joining technique that was devised by two prior students, Marie Rice and Roberta Demmer. This really is the perfect join technique for modern tatting.

You may also notice that I have changed certain terminology. Most notably, "stitch" has been replaced with "knot." The correct term for modern tatting is double knot.

Happy Tatting!

Teri Dusenbury

Symbols, Abbreviations and Explanations

Getting Started

All of the designs in this book are tatted using modern tatting techniques. In this style of tatting, precise manipulations of the shuttles are used throughout the pattern so that the lace will have a distinct front and back side. In other words, the bars of all the knots are facing the front of the lace.

One advantage to this modern style of tatting is eliminating having to turn the lace to the back just to tat a chain. By using one of two different knotting techniques (The Lark's Head Knot Chain or the Reverse Double Knot Chain), you eliminate the unnecessary hand movements required by traditional style of tatting chains.

The key elements to the success of any of the butterfly projects are good light, a quiet span of time, and patience. It is imperative that you thoroughly review all of the abbreviations, basics, and techniques before attempting to tat any of the motifs. Be sure to follow the written script while using the schematics.

CH/DK = Double Knot Chain. The bar of this chain knot is *above* the hitches. The hitches of the double knot chain are manipulated with shuttle 2's thread and transfer over to shuttle 1's thread. Use this chain only when specified in the directions.

CH or X = Lark's Head Knot Chain. The bar of this knot is *below* the hitches. The hitches are manipulated with shuttle 2's thread and are slid into place on shuttle 1's thread. There is no transference of the hitches. The lark's head knot is the second hitch, and then the first hitch worked in that order. The lark's head knot is manipulated while the lace is facing the front. There is no turning the lace to the back.

OR

CH or X = Reverse Double Knot Chain. The bar of this knot is *below* the hitches. The hitches are manipulated with the running thread (shuttle 1's thread) and transfer over to shuttle 2's or the ball's thread. The reverse double knot is the second hitch of the double knot, and then the first hitch of the double knot tatted in that order. The reverse double knot is manipulated while the lace is facing the front. There is no turning of the work to the back.

~<>—CTM—-<>~ = Continuous Thread Method. Using two shuttles, fill one shuttle and place that shuttle down. Pull enough thread off the ball to fill the second shuttle. Cut the thread from the ball and fill the second shuttle. You will be tatting from the center of the thread. This eliminates two thread ends that would have to be rethreaded into the lace upon completion. All butterfly motifs use this method.

DK = Double Knot. The bar of this knot is *above* the hitches. When tatting a ring, the hitches of the double knot are manipulated with the running thread (shuttle 1's thread) and transfer over to the ring thread. The double knot is the first hitch (under the ring thread), and then the second hitch (over the ring thread) tatted in that order.

DR = Directional Ring. Reverse the work so that the back of the lace is facing you. The sequence of the hitches is tatted in a precise formula. Instead of tatting the double knot, which would appear in the wrong sequence on the front of the lace, you start the ring with the *second* hitch of the double knot, then work the required number of double knots, minus one. End the sequence with the *first* hitch of the double knot. Guide the shuttle through the ring to the front of the work before closing the ring.

Directional Ring Join. When joining a directional ring, pull the ring thread up through the bottom of the picot until a loop large enough to pass the shuttle through is formed. Guide the shuttle through the top of the loop to the back. Pull the ring thread until the loop is taut. This is considered the second hitch in a directional ring.

☉ or DYK = Dora Young Knot. The bar of this knot is above the hitches. The shuttle and thread are manipulated so that a knot is formed on a fixed running thread. See page 30.

E = End.

+ or join. All joins (except for lock knot joins) are considered a knot and are calculated in the knot count. Pull the ring thread down through the top of the picot until a loop large enough to pass the shuttle through is formed. (When joining the lark's head knot or the reverse double knot to a picot, it is the ball or shuttle 2's thread that is pulled down through the top of the picot.) Guide the shuttle through the front of the loop to the back. Pull the ring thread until the loop is taut. This is the first hitch of the knot. Tat the second hitch of the double knot (the first hitch when tatting the lark's head knot or reverse double knot chains) to complete the knot.

- (dash) or LKP = Link Picot. A link picot is a tiny loop of thread.

LK = Lock Knot. The lock knot is used to lock the running (internal) thread in place. The lock knot is formed with the shuttle thread. The thread is pulled down through the top of the picot. The shuttle is slipped through the loop and then the loop is pulled taut. A lock knot does not count as any hitch or knot. The lock knot is used primarily in chain joins.

LP = Long picot.

MP = Medium picot.

P = Picot.

R = Ring.

RW = Reverse Work. Reverse or turn your lace to the back or wrong side of the lace. Reverse work is used primarily with directional rings.

S = Start.

SP = Small picot.

SR = Split Ring. A split ring is tatted with two shuttles. The top/first part of the ring is tatted with shuttle 1 using the double knot. The bottom/second part of the ring is tatted with shuttle 2 using the lark's head knot.

Split Ring Lark's Head Knot Join. When joining the second/bottom portion of a split ring using the lark's head knot to a chain or ring picot, pull the ring thread

up through the bottom of the picot until a loop large enough to pass the shuttle through is formed. Guide the shuttle through the top of the loop to the back. Pull the ring thread until the loop is taut. This is considered the second hitch. Tat the first hitch to complete the knot and join.

S1 = Shuttle one.

S2 = Shuttle two.

. (period) = Close ring or end of chain.

÷ = Separated by.

* = Indicates where the pattern repeat starts and ends.

● = Shuttle one bead.

Ɵ = Shuttle two bead

Ⓐ = Add on bead

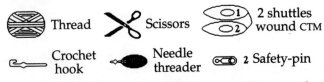

Pattern Script and Schematics

Instructions for all of the projects are written using an advanced condensed script format. It is suggested that both the written script and the companion schematic drawings be used together (rather than relying on one or the other) while tatting the basic butterfly motifs.

The following explanations will help you understand the format used.

R5-1, mp, 1-5. Translates to: use shuttle one to manipulate knots. Ring of five double knots, link picot, one double knot, medium picot, one double knot, link picot, five double knots, close ring. Place a safety-pin on shuttle two's thread. (*Fig. 1*)

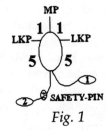

Fig. 1

CH/DK: 5+(R1)5, sp, 5. RW. Translates to: use shuttle two to manipulate knots. Tat a double knot chain of five double knots, join to picot of prior ring one, five double knots, one small picot, five double knots, end of chain. Reverse your work to face the back.

DR/S2: R7-7. Translates to: use shuttle two to manipulate knots. Ring of second hitch, six double knots, first hitch, link picot, second hitch, six double knots, first hitch, guide shuttle two through ring to front of lace, close ring. (*Fig. 2*)

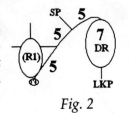

Fig. 2

Threads

The hardest decision may not be which project to tat first, but what threads to use. From silk to postal twine, and everything in between, may be used. There are only two rules to follow. First, don't combine fibers that are not compatible, especially if you plan to wash your project. Second, use fibers that are relatively smooth, so that the hitches aren't caught on "nubbies," making it impossible to close a ring. Have fun and experiment. Combine different gauges of cotton thread. Add filament threads to give your tatting sparkle or a burst of contrasting color.

Wind two size 80 threads together, or use a single strand of button and carpet thread for motifs meant for earrings or pins.

For larger motifs, experiment with sailing cord, macramé cords, or twine. Most of these cords are nylon and take a bit of strength and dexterity to keep the knots consistent; however, don't let that stop you from experimenting with these choices.

Yarn is also a viable alternative, as are pearl cottons, ribbons, embroidery floss, tapestry wool, etc.

Finishing Touches

Tie a square knot where two threads meet. Before cutting off the excess thread, rethread the ends back through the finished knots using a needle threader. Pull the ends through as many knots as possible before cutting off the excess thread. Be sure to rethread your ends before ironing any piece of lace. The heat from the iron dulls the thread, making it harder to slip the thread through the finished knots.

Lightly iron the work on the wrong side using a spray starch. For a firmer motif, use a commercial stiffener, being sure to follow the manufacturers directions.

Tatting Basics

The Reverse Riego Style of Shuttle Manipulation—The Double Knot

Pinch the shuttle thread between the thumb and index finger of the left hand. Wrap the thread that comes from the shuttle over the back of the left hand and back around to the thumb and index finger. Pinch both threads between the thumb and index finger to form a ring. The thread wrapped around your left hand is called the *ring thread*. The thread that comes out from under the thumb and is connected to the shuttle is called the *shuttle thread*.

The *first hitch* of the double knot is tatted by draping the shuttle thread over the middle finger of the left hand, behind the ring thread. Pointing the shuttle away from you, guide the shuttle from in front of the top ring thread, back between the middle and ring fingers of the left hand (*Fig. 3*).

Pull the shuttle to the right until the hitch "transfers over" (*Figs. 4 & 5*). Using the middle finger of your left hand, pull the hitch up and to the left, bringing the hitch taut (*Fig. 6*). This completes the first hitch. Hold the hitch under the thumb and index finger of your left hand.

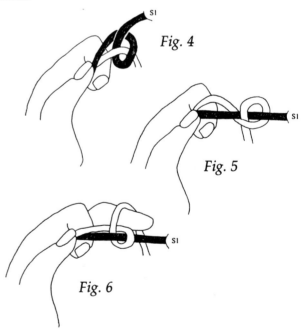

Fig. 4

Fig. 5

Fig. 6

The *second hitch* of the double knot is tatted by draping the shuttle thread in front of the ring thread. Pointing the shuttle towards you, guide the shuttle between the middle and ring fingers of the left hand from behind and under the ring thread to the front, yet still over the shuttle thread (*Fig. 7*).

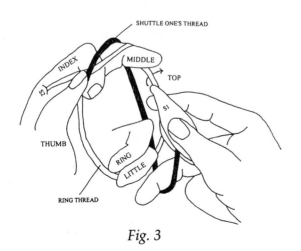

Fig. 3

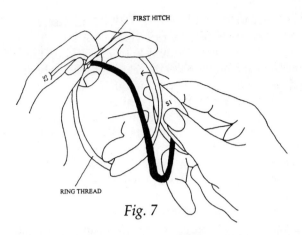

Fig. 7

Pull the shuttle thread to the right until the hitch transfers over. Using the middle finger of your left hand, pull the hitch up and to the left, bringing the hitch taut and next to the first hitch, completing the double stitch. (*Figs. 8 & 9*).

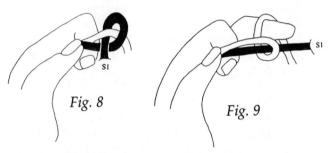

Fig. 8

Fig. 9

Fig. 10 shows how the double knot looks when tatted correctly. A good test is to pull the shuttle thread to see if the ring thread still moves freely. If the thread does not move, then a mistake has been made.

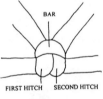

Fig. 10

Picots

Picots are loops of thread that rest on top of the knots. They are easily made by leaving a space between the last hitch of one knot and the first hitch of the next knot (*Fig. 11*).

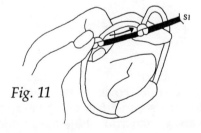

Fig. 11

Joins

All joins except for lock knot joins are considered knots and are calculated in the knot count.

Ring joins are made by pulling the ring thread down through the top of the picot until a loop large enough

to pass the shuttle through is formed. Guide the shuttle through the top of the loop to the back (*Fig. 12*). Pull the ring thread until the loop is taut. This is the first hitch of the knot. Tat the second hitch of the double knot to complete the join (*Fig. 13*).

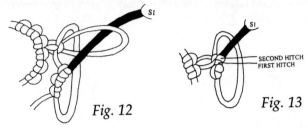

Fig. 12

Fig. 13

Joining the last ring's picot to the first ring's picot is made by removing the lace from your left hand. Turn ring A so that its first picot is facing towards you. Place the ring thread of the uncompleted ring over the first picot of ring A. Using a crochet hook, pull thread down through the top of the first picot of ring A until a loop large enough to pass the shuttle through is formed. Guide the shuttle through the top of the loop to the back. Pull the ring thread until the loop is taut (*Figs. 14 & 15*). This is the first hitch of the knot join. Tat the second hitch of the double knot to complete the join and the knot (*Fig. 16*).

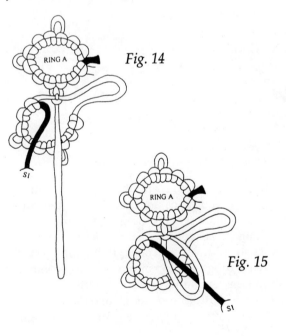

Fig. 14

Fig. 15

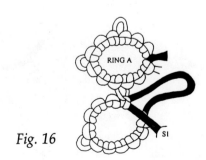

Fig. 16

Directional Ring joins are made by pulling the ring thread *up* through the bottom of the picot until a loop large enough to pass the shuttle through is formed. Guide the shuttle through the top of the loop to the back (*Fig. 17*). Pull the ring thread until the loop is taut. This is considered the second hitch in a directional ring join (*Fig. 18*).

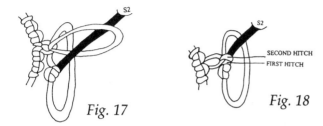

Fig. 17

Fig. 18

Split Ring–Lark's Head Knot joins are made when joining the second/bottom portion of a split ring using the lark's head knot to a chain or ring picot. Pull the ring thread up through the bottom of the picot until a loop large enough to pass the shuttle through is formed. Guide the shuttle through the top of the loop to the back (*Fig. 19*). Pull the ring thread until the loop is taut. This is considered the second hitch. Tat the first hitch to complete the join and the knot (*Fig. 20*).

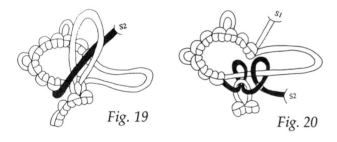

Fig. 19

Fig. 20

Lock knot joins are made with the running or internal thread. Lock knot joins are used to lock the running thread into place when joining a chain to a picot. Lock knot joins do *not* count as a hitch or knot, nor are they calculated in any knot count. Pull shuttle one's thread down through the top of the picot to be joined until a loop large enough to pass the shuttle through is formed. Guide shuttle one through and then pull the loop taut by continuing to pull the shuttle to the right (*Fig. 21*).

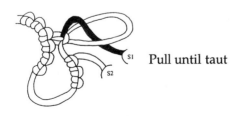

Pull until taut

Fig. 21

The Reverse Double Knot Chain

It is no longer necessary to reverse your lace just to tat chains. The reverse double knot consists of the two hitches that comprise the double knot. The only difference is the order in which the hitches are tatted—the second hitch and then the first hitch. The hitches of the reverse double knot are made with the ball thread and are carried upon the shuttle's thread. The tricky part of the reverse double knot is getting the starting chain hitch taut and close to the base of the ring; this hitch may take a bit more manipulation to place than consecutive hitches.

DO NOT REVERSE YOUR WORK! Wrap the ball thread (S2's thread) around your hand, securing the thread to the little finger (just as you would have secured the thread if you had reversed your work to tat your chain). Shuttle one's thread crosses in front of the secured ball thread (or S2's thread). Instead of tatting the first hitch of the double knot, you tat the second hitch. The shuttle thread crosses over in front of the secured ball/S2's thread. The first hitch of the reverse double knot is made by pointing the shuttle towards you, guiding the shuttle between the third and ring fingers of the left hand from behind and under the chain thread to the front, yet still over the shuttle thread. Pull the shuttle to the right until the hitch "transfers" over (just like the hitches do when tatting the double knot). Using the middle finger of your left hand, pull the ball (S2's) thread down and taut, forcing the hitch to slide to the left, bringing the hitch taut next to the base of the last ring tatted. This is referred to as the *first hitch* of the reverse double knot (*Figs. 22 & 23*).

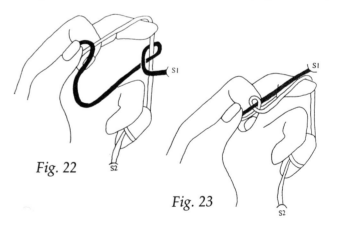

Fig. 22

Fig. 23

For the second hitch of the reverse double knot, drape the shuttle thread over the third finger of the left hand, behind the secured ball (S2's) thread. Pointing the shuttle away from you, guide the shuttle from in front of and under the chain thread, back between the third and ring fingers of the left hand. Pull shuttle one to the right until the hitch transfers over and is made with the ball's (S2's) thread. Using the middle finger of your left hand, pull the ball (S2's) thread down and taut, forcing the hitch to slide to the left, bringing the hitch taut next to the first hitch tatted. This is referred to as the *second hitch* of the reverse double knot (*Figs. 24 & 25*).

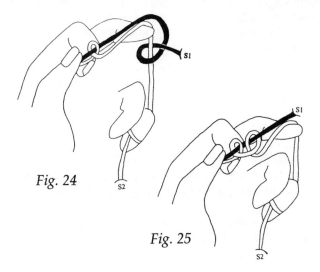

Fig. 24

Fig. 25

The Lark's Head Knot Chain

The lark's head knot chain is another alternative to traditional chain tatting. It is no longer necessary to reverse your lace just to tat chains. If you find the reverse double knot too difficult and time consuming to use while tatting chains, the lark's head knot is far easier to manipulate. Unlike the reverse double knot, which is a true tatting knot, the lark's head knot is a macramé knot. The hitches of the lark's head knot are made with the initial manipulating thread (S2's thread) and are not transferred over to the running

thread (S1's thread), but are slid into place upon the running thread. *There is no transference of the hitches to make the lark's head knot (Fig. 26).*

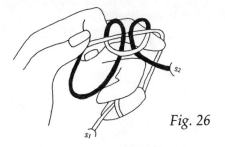

Fig. 26

The Double Knot Chain

The hitches that comprise the knot for the double knot chain are manipulated in the same sequence as you would while tatting a double knot for a ring. The only difference between the ring double knot and the chain double knot is the shuttle used to manipulate the hitches prior to transferring them over. In chain tatting with the double knot, the hitches are manipulated with the second shuttle's thread and transfer over to the first shuttle's thread (*Fig. 27*).

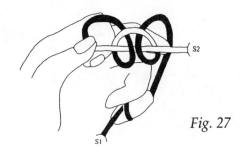

Fig. 27

Tatting Techniques

Split Ring Tatting

A split ring is a ring tatted with two shuttles. The top/first part of the ring is tatted with shuttle one using the double knot. The bottom/second portion of the ring is tatted with shuttle two using the lark's head knot (*Fig. 28*).

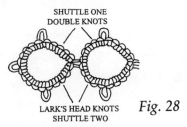

SHUTTLE ONE
DOUBLE KNOTS

LARK'S HEAD KNOTS
SHUTTLE TWO

Fig. 28

Use two shuttles wound CTM. The script reads: SR/S1: R5-5, S2: 5-5. Tat the first part of the split ring with shuttle one: SR/S1: R5-5.

S2: 5-5. The bottom/second part of the split ring is always tatted using the lark's head knot. The lark's head knot does not transfer over like the reverse double knot, but is made with the manipulating thread or the second shuttle's thread and slid into place.

The first hitch of the lark's head knot is knotted by pointing the shuttle towards you, guiding the shuttle behind and under the ring's thread, yet still over the second shuttle's thread. Pull the shuttle down and to the left, being careful *not* to transfer the hitch, but sliding the hitch next to the first double knot tatted (*Fig. 29, see next page*).

The second hitch of the lark's head knot is knotted by draping the shuttle thread over the fingers of the left hand. Pointing the shuttle away from you, guide the shuttle from in front of and under the ring thread. Bring the shuttle back over the top of the ring thread, yet still under the shuttle's thread. Pull the shuttle down and to the left, being careful not to transfer the hitch, but sliding the hitch next to the first hitch of the lark's head knot (*Fig. 30*).

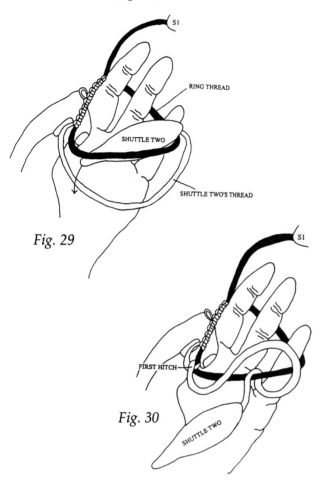

Fig. 29

Fig. 30

Directional Tatting

When you reverse your work and tat a double knot, the hitches are in reverse order on the front of your lace. With directional tatting, you tat the first and second hitches of the double knot in reverse order to achieve a complete double knot on the front of your lace.

The double knot consists of two hitches: the first hitch (the shuttle guided under the ring thread) and the second hitch (the shuttle guided over the ring thread). When you reverse your work, the double knot is seen as the second hitch followed by the first hitch (*Fig. 31*).

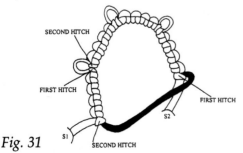

Fig. 31

Patterns that utilize directional ring tatting show the script written *as the stitches will appear on the front of the lace*. The key is **RW DR/S2:**, which requires you to follow the formula given below in order to have all the knots facing the front of the lace.

The best way to understand directional tatting is by tatting the following example.

R5-1-1-5. This ring will give you something to hold onto.

Butt:
CH/DK: 5. RW
DR/S2: R5-5. RW You will need to break that first sequence of knots down in your mind to read second hitch, four complete double knots, first hitch. It is helpful to remember that each sequence starts with the second hitch, ends with the first hitch, and the number of complete double knots is one less than the total number. This is how the pattern script would read if it were written to show how the hitches and knots would appear on the reverse side of the lace. DR/S2: R2h, 4 dk, 1h-2h, 4 dk, 1h. RW Remember to bring the shuttle through the ring to the true front before closing the ring.

CH/DK: 5. RW
DR/S2: R7-7. RW Tat the second hitch, six complete double knots, first hitch, leave a small thread space of a link picot, second hitch, six complete double knots, first hitch, bring shuttle through the ring to the true front before closing the ring. RW
CH/DK: 5. RW
DR/S2: R5-5. RW
CH/DK: 10+(lk, last R4)5+(lk, next R3)5+(lk, next R2)5+(lk in space between first ring and first chain knot). End off (*Fig. 32*).

Fig. 32

Stacking

Stacking is a technique in which you tat rings one on top of the other to achieve a three-dimensional effect. The best way to learn how to stack is to tat the following butterfly example.

~<>—ball
Butt: (*Fig. 33*)
R5-5, sp, 1, mp, 1, sp, 5-5.

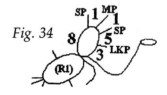

Fig. 33

Upper left small wing:
(*Fig. 34*)
R8, sp, 1, mp, 1, sp, 5-3.
Fold this ring down so that
the back side is facing up.

Fig. 34

Lower left small wing:
(*Fig. 35*)
R5+(last p, R1)3, sp, 1, mp, 1, sp, 5-3.
Push the second ring in front of the third ring.

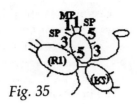

Fig. 35

Upper left large wing:
(*Fig. 36*)
R3+(last p, R2)5, sp, 1, mp, 1, lp, 10-3.
Fold both connected wings down so that the back side is facing up.

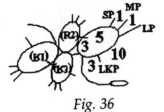

Fig. 36

Lower left large wing:
(*Fig. 37*)
R3+(last p, R3)5, sp, 1, mp, 1, lp, 10-3.
Fold both connected wings up so that they are stacked on each other.

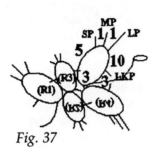

Fig. 37

Head: (*Fig. 38*)
R3+(last p's of R4 and R5)1, mp, 1-3.

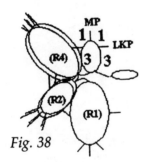

Fig. 38

Lower right large wing:
(*Fig. 39*)
R3+(last p, R6)10, lp, 1, mp, 1, sp, 5-3.

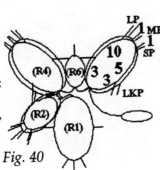

Fig. 39

Upper right large wing:
(*Fig. 40*)
R3+(last p, R6)10, lp, 1, mp, 1, sp, 5-3.
End off.

Fig. 40

Lower right small wing:
(*Fig. 41*)
R3+(last p, R7)5, sp, 1, mp, 1, sp, 3-5.

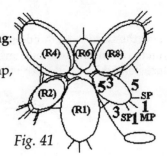

Fig. 41

Upper right small wing:
(*Fig. 42*)
R3+(last p, R8)5, sp, 1, mp, 1, sp, 8.
End off.

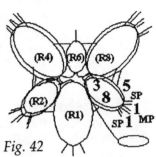

Fig. 42

Beading

Tatting with beads can be easy and a beautiful way in which to embellish your tatted lace.

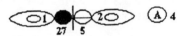

Before winding any shuttles, add the bead count together: 27 + 5 = 32 beads. Place thirty-two beads onto ball thread. Wind shuttle one. Pull enough thread from ball to fill second shuttle. Wind shuttle two. Divide the bead count as follows:
Shuttle one's thread holds twenty-seven beads.
● = shuttle one bead.
Shuttle two's thread holds five beads.
⊖ = shuttle two bead.
There are four additional, yet separate, add-on beads that are placed on picots.
Ⓐ = add on bead

If the bead is placed in the ring's picot, the bead must be first slid into the ring before tatting the first knot of the ring (*Fig. 43*).
If the bead is placed among the ring's knots, then the bead is slid from shuttle one at the appropriate time for placement (*Fig. 44*).

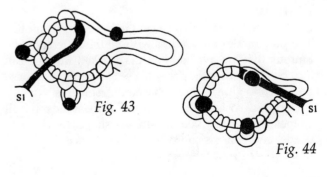

Fig. 43

Fig. 44

If the bead is an "add-on" bead, the picot should be made the appropriate length, not only to accomodate the bead, but to allow for the join thread too (*Fig. 45*).

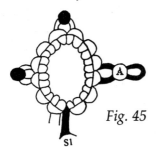

Fig. 45

Embellishments

Each of the butterfly motifs can be suspended on a tatted split ring neck chain or used alone as a pin, earrings, or a hair ornament, or appliquéd onto clothing, hats, purses, and even shoes.

Buttons, baubles, beads, rhinestones, ribbon roses, Brazilian embroidery flowers, silk flowers, porcelain flowers, quilled flowers, pearls, semi-precious stones, cabochons, sequins, crystal hearts, charms, and lockets can all be used as embellishments. Let your imagination loose and create your own unique butterfly motif.

Ribbon Rosettes

Ribbon rosettes are simple to make. The width of the ribbon depends upon the size thread used to tat the butterfly. You'll need approximately 5½ inches of ribbon, sewing thread, needle, and one appropriately-sized bead to make one rosette.

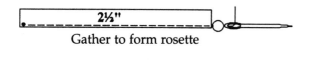

Gather to form rosette

Fold and tack together to form bow

Place rosette on bow and tack

Buttons

Buttons are a great enhancement to the butterfly motifs. The possibilities are endless with all the different style buttons that are available on the market. Buttons can also be used, after they're sewn onto a motif, as a base on which to glue non-sewable embellishments.

Ceramic roses, ribbon roses, rhinestones in all shapes and sizes, sequins in all shapes and sizes, beads, and charms can be used to enhance the center of any of the motifs.

Use your favorite brand of tacky glue or use a hot glue gun to attach embellishments to a button base.

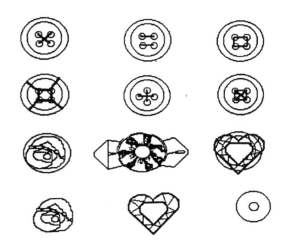

Findings

All of the motifs, when tatted in a finer thread (70, 80, 100) will make wonderful earrings, whether suspended from fish hook wires or glued onto flathead posts.

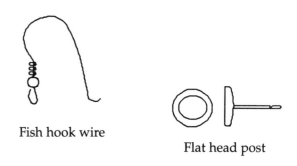

Fish hook wire

Flat head post

Lobster claw clasps can be used as an alternative to a neck chain that merely slips over one's head. Clasps should be used when tatting split ring bracelets or chokers.

All of the motifs would make wonderful pins. Sew or glue onto a bar pin or rounded bar pin finding.

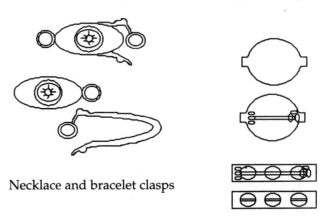

Necklace and bracelet clasps

Pin findings

Novice Butterfly

Materials: Thread, scissors, 1 shuttle, crochet hook, needle threader.

~<>—

Butt: (*Fig. 1*)
R5-5, sp, 1, mp, 1, sp, 5-5.

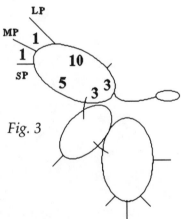

Fig. 1

Left small wing: (*Fig. 2*)
R5+(last p, R1)3, sp, 5-3.

Fig. 2

Right large wing: (*Fig. 5*)
R3+(last p, R4) 10, lp, 1, mp, 1, sp, 5-3.

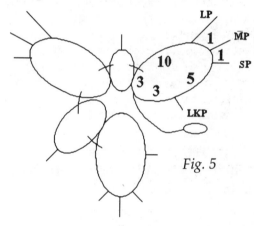

Fig. 5

Left large wing: (*Fig. 3*)
R3+(last p, R2) 5, sp, 1,
mp, 1, lp, 10-3.

Fig. 3

Right small wing: (*Fig. 6*)
R3+(last p, R5)5, sp, 3+(first p, R1)5. End off.
Tie a square knot on wrong side of lace.

Head: (*Fig. 4*)
R3+(last p, R3) 1,
mp, 1-3.

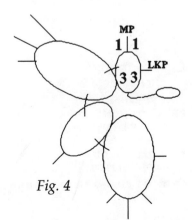

Fig. 4

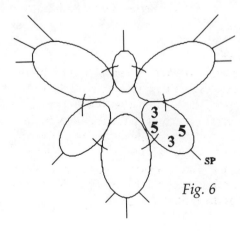

Fig. 6

Butterfly #1

Materials: Thread, scissors, 2 shuttles wound CTM, crochet hook, needle threader, 2 small safety-pins.

~<>——CTM——<>~

Head: (*Fig. 1*)
R5-1, mp, 1-5. Place safety-pin on S2's thread.

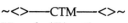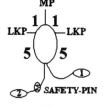

Fig. 1

Right small wing: (*Fig. 4*)
CH/DK: 5+(last chain p)3.
*R4, sp, 4.
CH/DK: 2* 2xs.
R4, sp, 4.
CH/DK: 3-5+(remove safety-pin and join in space with a lock knot). Place safety-pin back on S2's thread.

Right large wing: (*Figs. 2 & 3*)
CH/DK: 5+(R1)5, sp, 5. RW
DR/S2: R7-7. RW
CH/DK: 5.
R4, sp, 4.
*CH/DK: 2.
R4, sp, 4. *3xs.
CH/DK: 5+(lk, R2)5-5+(remove safety-pin and join in space with a lock knot). Place safety-pin back on S2's thread.

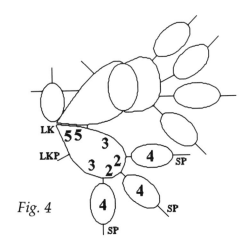

Fig. 4

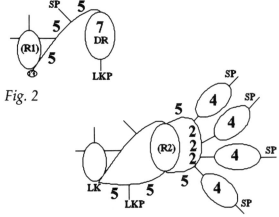

Fig. 2

Fig. 3

(R1) = RING ONE
DR = DIRECTIONAL RING
LKP = LINK PICOT
LK = LOCK KNOT
SP = SMALL PICOT
MP = MEDIUM PICOT

NOTE: ALL CHAINS ARE DOUBLE KNOT CHAINS.

Butt: (*Fig. 5*)
CH/DK: 5. RW
DR/S2: R5-5. RW
CH/DK: +(last chain p)5. RW
DR/S2: R7-7. RW
CH/DK: 5. RW
DR/S2: R5-5. RW
CH/DK: 10+(lk, last R12)5+(lk, next R11)5 +(lk, next R10)5+(remove safety-pin and join in space with a lock knot). Place safety-pin back on S2's thread.

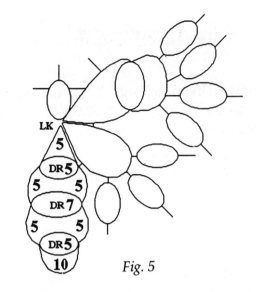

Fig. 5

Left small wing: (*Fig. 6*)
CH/DK: 5+(last ring's lk join space)3.
*R4, sp, 4.
CH/DK: 2* 2xs.
R4, sp, 4.
CH/DK: 3-5+(remove safety-pin and join in space with a lock knot). Place safety-pin back on S2's thread.

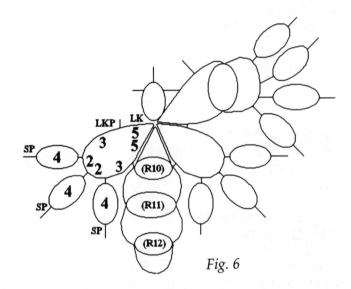

Fig. 6

Left large wing: (*Fig. 7*)
CH/DK: 5+(last chain p)5(place safety-pin on S2's thread)5.
*R4, sp, 4.
CH/DK: 2.* 3xs.
R4, sp, 4.
CH/DK: 5. RW
DR/S2: R7+(remove safety-pin and join in space)7. RW
CH/DK: 5, sp, 5+(first p, R1)5. End off. Remove safety-pin and join S2's thread in space with a lock knot. Pull S2's thread through space between base of R1 and first chain knot. Tie a square knot on wrong side of lace.

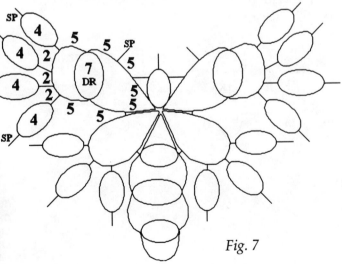

Fig. 7

15

Butterfly #2

Materials: Thread, scissors, 2 shuttles wound CTM, crochet hook, needle threader, 1 small safety-pin.

~<>——CTM——<>~

Head: (*Fig. 1*)
R5-1, mp, 1-5. Place safety-pin on S2's thread.

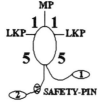

Fig. 1

Right large wing: (*Fig. 2*)
CH/DK: 5+(R1)20.
R4, sp, 4.
*CH/DK: 2.
R4, sp, 4.* 2xs
CH/DK: 5-5+(remove safety-pin and join in space with a lock knot). Place safety-pin back on S2's thread.

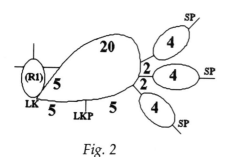

Fig. 2

Right small wing: (*Fig. 3*)
CH/DK: 5+(last chain p)10.
R4, sp, 4.
CH/DK: 2.
R4, sp, 4.
CH/DK: 5-5+(remove safety-pin and join in space with a lock knot). Place safety-pin back on S2's thread.

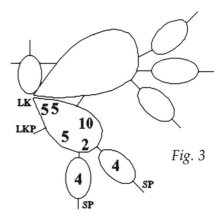

Fig. 3

(R1) = RING ONE
DR = DIRECTIONAL RING
LKP = LINK PICOT
LK = LOCK KNOT
SP = SMALL PICOT
MP = MEDIUM PICOT

NOTE: ALL CHAINS ARE DOUBLE KNOT CHAINS.

Butt: (*Fig. 4*)
CH/DK: 5. RW
DR/S2: R5-5. RW
CH/DK: +(last chain p)5. RW
DR/S2: R7-7. RW
CH/DK: 5. RW
DR/S2: R5-5. RW
CH/DK: 10+(lk, last R9)5+(lk, next R8)5+(lk, next R7)5+(remove safety-pin and join in space with a lock knot). Place safety-pin back on S2's thread.

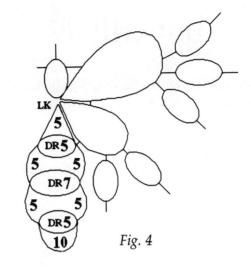

Fig. 4

Left small wing: (*Fig. 5*)
CH/DK: 5+(last ring's lk join space)5.
R4, sp, 4.
CH/DK: 2.
R4, sp, 4.
CH/DK: 10-5+(remove safety-pin and join in space with a lock knot). Place safety-pin back on S2's thread.

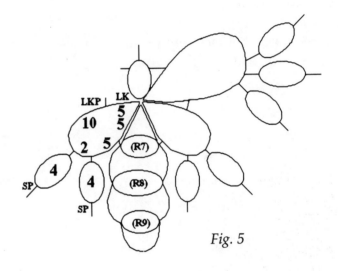

Fig. 5

Left large wing: (*Fig. 6*)
CH/DK: 5+(last chain p)5.
*R4, sp, 4.
CH/DK: 2.* 2xs
R4, sp, 4.
CH/DK: 20+(first p, R1)5. End off. Remove safety-pin and join S2's thread in space with a lock knot. Pull S2's thread through space between base of R1 and first chain knot. Tie a square knot on wrong side of lace.

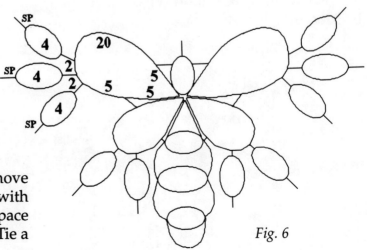

Fig. 6

Butterfly #3

Materials: Thread, scissors, 2 shuttles wound CTM, crochet hook, needle threader, 3 small safety-pins.

~<>——CTM——<>~

Head: (*Fig. 1*)
R5-1, mp, 1-5. Place safety-pin on S2's thread.

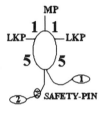

Fig. 1

Right small wing: (*Fig. 4*)
CH/DK: 5+(last chain p)5. RW
DR/S2: R5-5. RW
CH/DK: 2, five sp separated by 2+(lk, R4)5-5+(remove safety-pin and join in space with a lock knot). Place safety-pin back on S2's thread.

Right large wing: (*Figs. 2 & 3*)
CH/DK: 5+(R1)10. RW
DR/S2: R7-7. RW
CH/DK: 5. RW
DR/S2: R5-5. RW
CH/DK: 2, five sp separated by 2+(lk, R3)2, sp, 3+(lk, R2)5-5+(remove safety-pin and join in space with a lock knot). Place safety-pin back on S2's thread.

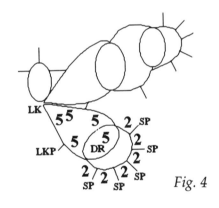

Fig. 4

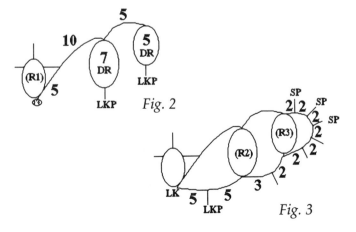

Fig. 2

Fig. 3

(R1) = RING ONE
DR = DIRECTIONAL RING
LKP = LINK PICOT
LK = LOCK KNOT
SP = SMALL PICOT
MP = MEDIUM PICOT

NOTE: ALL CHAINS ARE DOUBLE KNOT CHAINS.

Butt: (*Fig. 5*)
CH/DK: 5. RW
DR/S2: R5-5. RW
CH/DK: +(last chain p)5. RW
DR/S2: R7-7. RW
CH/DK: 5. RW
DR/S2: R5-5. RW
CH/DK: 10+(lk, last R7)5+(lk, next R6)5+(lk, next R5)5+(remove safety-pin and join in space with a lock knot). Place safety-pin back on S2's thread.

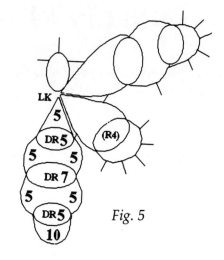

Fig. 5

Left small wing: (*Fig. 6*)
CH/DK: 5+(last ring's lk join space)5(place safety-pin on S2's thread)2, five sp separated by 2. RW
DR/S2: R5+(remove second safety-pin and join in space)5. RW
CH/DK: 5-5+(remove safety-pin and join in space with a lock knot). Place safety-pin back on S2's thread.

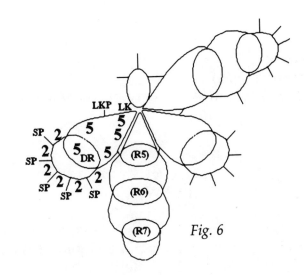

Fig. 6

Left large wing: (*Fig. 7*)
CH/DK: 5+(last chain p)5(place safety-pin on S2's thread)3, sp, 2(place another safety-pin on S2's thread)2, five sp separated by 2. RW
DR/S2: R5+(remove third safety-pin and join in space)5. RW
CH/DK: 5. RW
DR/S2: R7+(remove second safety-pin and join in space)7. RW
CH/DK: 10+(first p, R1)5. End off.
Remove safety-pin and join S2's thread in space with a lock knot. Pull S2's thread through space between base of R1 and first chain knot. Tie a square knot on wrong side of lace.

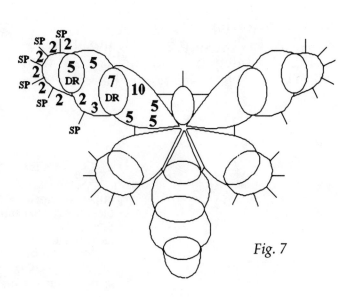

Fig. 7

Butterfly #4

Materials: Thread, scissors, 2 shuttles wound CTM, crochet hook, needle threader, 3 safety-pins.

~<>—-CTM—-<>~
Head: (*Fig. 1*)
R5-1, mp, 1-5. Place safety-pin on S2's thread.

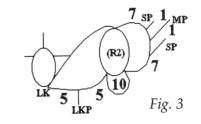

Fig. 1

Right large wing: (*Figs. 2 & 3*)
CH/DK: 5+(R1)10. RW
DR/S2: R5-5-5. RW
CH/DK: 7, sp, 1, mp, 1, sp, 7+(lk, R2)10+(lk, R2)5-5+(remove safety-pin and join in space with lock knot). Place safety-pin back on S2's thread.

Fig. 2   *Fig. 3*

Right small wing: (*Fig. 4*)
CH/DK: 5+(last ch p)5, sp, 1, mp, 1, sp, 5-5+(remove safety-pin and join in space with lock knot). Place safety-pin back on S2's thread.

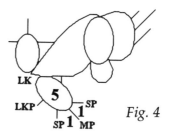

Fig. 4

(R1) = RING ONE
DR = DIRECTIONAL RING
LKP = LINK PICOT
LK = LOCK KNOT
SP = SMALL PICOT
MP = MEDIUM PICOT

NOTE: ALL CHAINS ARE DOUBLE KNOT CHAINS.

Butt: (*Fig. 5*)
CH/DK: 5. RW
DR/S2: R5-5. RW
CH/DK: +(last chain p)5. RW
DR/S2: R7-7. RW
CH/DK: 5. RW
DR/S2: R5-5. RW
CH/DK: 10+(lk, last R5)5+(lk, next R4)5+(lk, next R3)5+(remove safety-pin and join in space with lock knot). Place safety-pin back on S2's thread.

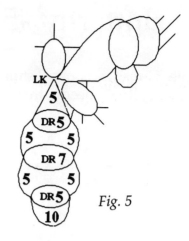

Fig. 5

Left small wing: (*Fig. 6*)
CH/DK: 5+(last ring's lk join space), 5, sp, 1, mp, 1, sp, 5-5+(remove safety-pin and join in space with lock knot). Place safety-pin back on S2's thread.

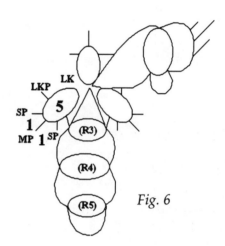

Fig. 6

Left large wing: (*Fig. 7*)
CH/DK: 5+(last ch p)5(place another safety-pin on S2's thread)10(place another safety-pin on S2's thread)7, sp, 1, mp, 1, sp, 7. RW
DR/S2: R5+(remove third safety-pin and join in space)5+(remove second safety-pin and join in space)5. RW
CH/DK: 10+(first p, R1)5. End off.
Remove first safety-pin and join S2's thread in space with a lock knot. Pull S2's thread through space between base of R1 and first chain knot. Tie a square knot on wrong side of lace.

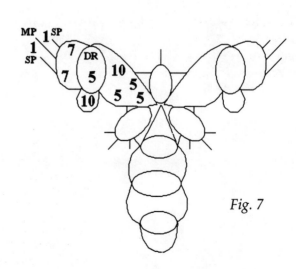

Fig. 7

Butterfly #5

Materials: Thread, scissors, 2 shuttles wound CTM, crochet hook, needle threader, 2 small safety-pins.

Head: (*Fig. 1*)
R5-1, mp, 1-5. Place safety-pin on S2's thread.

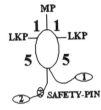

Fig. 1

Right small wing: (*Fig. 4*)
CH/DK: 5+(last chain p)5. RW
DR/S2: R5-5. RW
CH/DK: 10+(lk, R4),
R4, sp, 4.
CH/DK: 5-5+(remove safety-pin and join in space with a lock knot). Place safety-pin back on S2's thread.

Right large wing: (*Figs. 2 & 3*)
CH/DK: 5+(R1)10. RW
DR/S2: R7-7. RW
CH/DK: 15+(lk, R2),
R4, sp, 4.
CH/DK: 5-5+(remove safety-pin and join in space with a lock knot). Place safety-pin back on S2's thread.

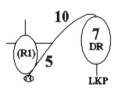

Fig. 2

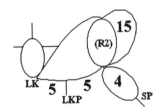

Fig. 3

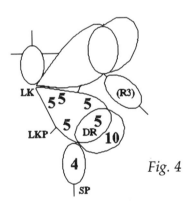

Fig. 4

(R1) = RING ONE
DR = DIRECTIONAL RING
LKP = LINK PICOT
LK = LOCK KNOT
SP = SMALL PICOT
MP = MEDIUM PICOT

NOTE: ALL CHAINS ARE DOUBLE KNOT CHAINS.

Butt: (*Fig. 5*)
CH/DK: 5. RW
DR/S2: R5-5. RW
CH/DK: +(last chain p)5. RW
DR/S2: R7-7. RW
CH/DK: 5. RW
DR/S2: R5-5. RW
CH/DK: 10+(lk, last R8)5+(lk, next R7)5+(lk, next R6)5+(remove safety-pin and join in space with a lock knot). Place safety-pin back on S2's thread.

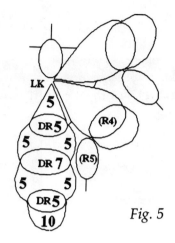

Fig. 5

Left small wing: (*Fig. 6*)
CH/DK: 5+(last ring's lk join space)5(place another safety-pin on S2's thread), R4, sp, 4.
CH/DK: 10. RW
DR/S2: R5+(remove second safety-pin and join in space)5. RW
CH/DK: 5-5+(remove safety-pin and join in space with a lock knot). Place safety-pin back on S2's thread.

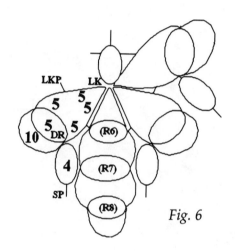

Fig. 6

Left large wing: (*Fig. 7*)
CH/DK: 5+(last chain p)5(place another safety-pin on S2's thread).
R4, sp, 4.
CH/DK: 15. RW
DR/S2: R7+(remove second safety-pin and join in space)7. RW
CH/DK: 10+(first p, R1)5. End off.
Remove safety-pin and join S2's thread in space with a lock knot. Pull S2's thread through space between base of R1 and first chain knot. Tie a square knot on wrong side of lace.

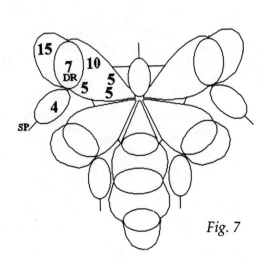

Fig. 7

23

Design Variations

Butterfly #1A

Butterfly #1B

Butterfly #2A

Butterfly #2B

Butterfly #1A

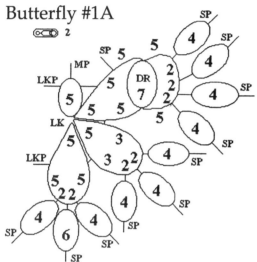

Butterfly #2A

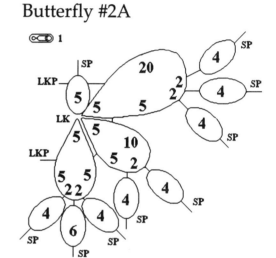

Butterfly #1B

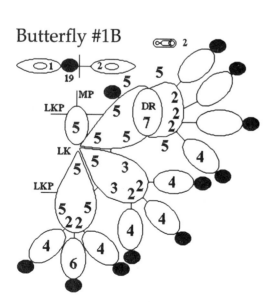

Butterfly #2B

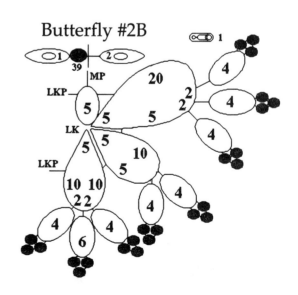

Butterfly #3A

Butterfly #3B

Butterfly #4A

Butterfly #4B

Butterfly #3A

 3

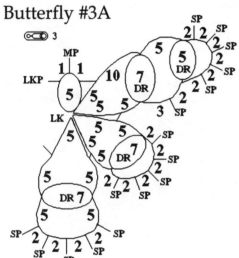

Butterfly #4A

3

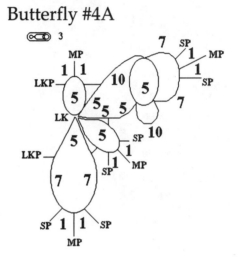

Butterfly #3B

3

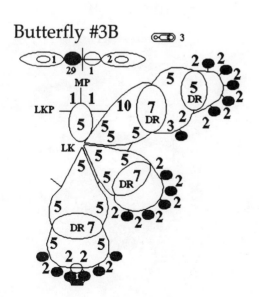

Butterfly #4B

3

Ⓐ 4

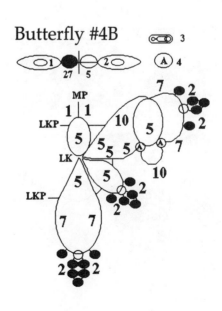

25

Butterfly #5A

Butterfly #5B

Novice Butterfly A

Novice Butterfly B

Butterfly #5A

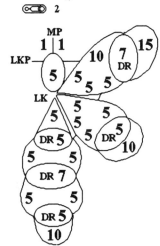

Novice Butterfly A

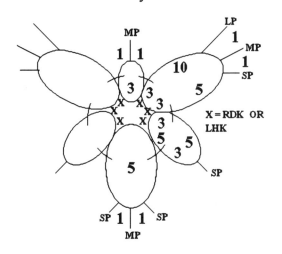

Butterfly #5B

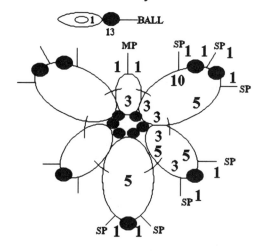

Novice Butterfly B

Split Ring Chain Variations

Materials: Thread, scissors, 2 shuttles wound CTM, crochet hook, needle threader, beads.

Note: Bead count depends upon length of chain.

These chain variation can be used for necklaces, chokers or bracelets.

Split Ring Chain A

Split Ring Chain B

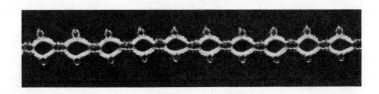

Split Ring Chain C

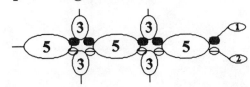

Split Ring Chain D

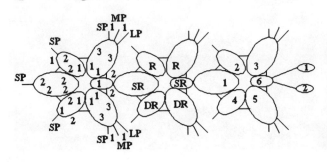

Tatbit in Flight Charmer Chatelaine

Materials: Thread, scissors, 2 shuttles wound CTM, crochet hook, needle threader.

Note: Use triple thread or a thicker thread (#5 at least) for chatelaine.

Tatbit

~<>——CTM——<>~

Inner body: (*Fig. 1*)
R2-2-2-2-2.

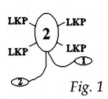

Fig. 1

Right leg: (*Figs. 6 & 7*)
CH/DK: 6,
R6, sp, 6.
CH/DK: 6+(work one more Dora Young Knot in second picot of R1)2+(work one Dora Young Knot in third picot of R1.)

Head: (*Figs. 2 & 3*)
R3-3, sp, 1, mp, 1, lp, 1, mp, 1, sp, 3-3.
CH/DK: 2+(work one Dora Young Knot (*see page 30*) in first picot of R1.)

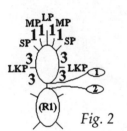 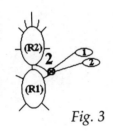

Fig. 2   *Fig. 3*

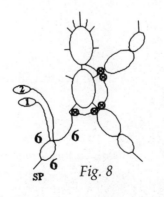

Fig. 6   *Fig. 7*

Right arm: (*Figs. 4 & 5*)
CH/DK: 3,
R4, sp, 6.
CH/DK: 3+(work one more Dora Young Knot in first picot of R1)2+(work one Dora Young Knot in second picot of R1.)

Left leg: (*Figs. 8 & 9*)
CH/DK: 6,
R6, sp, 6.
CH/DK: 6+(work one more Dora Young Knot in third picot of R1)2+(work one Dora Young Knot in fourth picot of R1.)

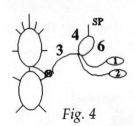 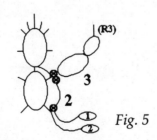

Fig. 4   *Fig. 5*

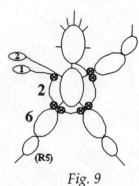

Fig. 8   *Fig. 9*

NOTE: ALL CHAINS ARE DOUBLE KNOT CHAINS.

⊗ = DORA YOUNG KNOT   MP = MEDIUM PICOT
LKP = LINK PICOT   SP = SMALL PICOT
LP = LONG PICOT   (R1) = RING ONE

The Dora Young Knot Technique

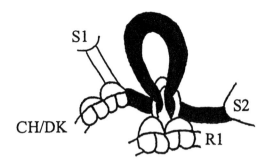

Step A. Pull shuttle two's thread up through the bottom of the picot. Pass shuttle two through the loop to the front, making sure that the loop does not twist.

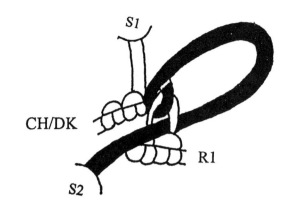

Step D.

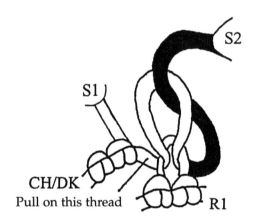

Step B. Pull on the thread that comes out from the base of the last double knot tatted until the loop and shuttle thread are pulled back through the picot.

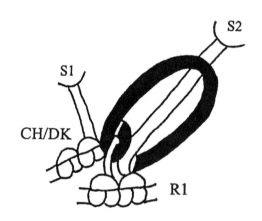

Step E. Pass shuttle two through the loop and pull on it to tighten the hitch.

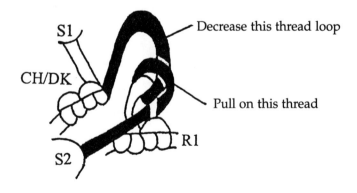

Step C. Pull on the bar thread to slide the hitch over to the left as shown in Step D.

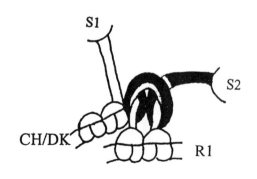

Step F. Completed DYK.

Left arm: (*Figs. 10 & 11*)
CH/DK: 3,
R6, sp, 4.
CH/DK: 3+(work one more Dora Young Knot in fourth picot of R1)2. End off. Bring S1's thread through space between R1 and R2. Tie a square knot on wrong side of lace.

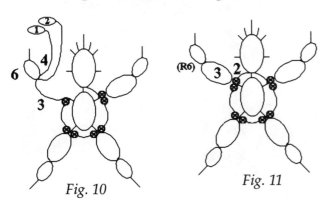

Fig. 10   Fig. 11

Butterfly #1

~<>—CTM—<>~
Butt: (*Fig. 12*)
R2-2+(p, R3-Tatbit)2-2.
CH/DK: 1,

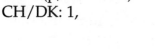

Fig. 12

Left small wing: (*Fig. 13*)
R2+(last p)1, sp, 2-1.
CH/DK:1,

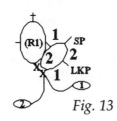

Fig. 13

Left large wing: (*Fig. 14*)
R1+(last p)3, sp, 1, mp, 1, lp, 3-1.
CH/DK: 1,

Fig. 14

Head: (*Fig. 15*)
R1+(last p)2, sp, 2-1.
CH/DK: 1,

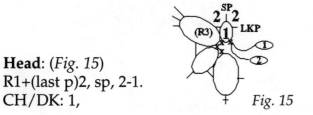

Fig. 15

Right large wing: (*Fig. 16*)
R1+(last p)3, lp, 1, mp, 1, sp, 3-1.
CH/DK: 1,

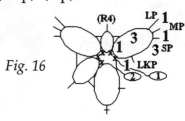

Fig. 16

Right small wing: (*Figs. 17 & 18*)
R1+(last p)2, sp, 1+(first p, R1)2.
CH/DK: 1. End off.
Bring S1's thread through space between base of R1 and first chain knot. Tie a square knot on wrong side of lace.

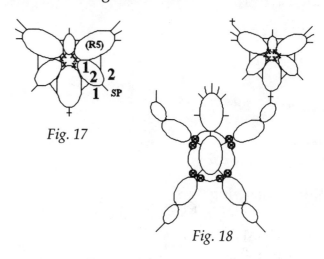

Fig. 17   Fig. 18

Butterfly #2 (*Fig. 19*)

~<>—ball
Butt:
R2-2+(lk, left large wing of butterfly #1)2-2.
CH/DK: 1,

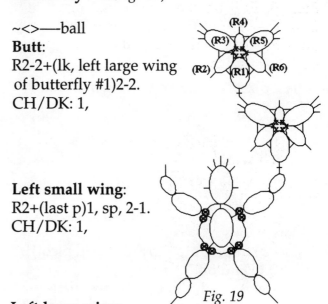

Left small wing:
R2+(last p)1, sp, 2-1.
CH/DK: 1,

Fig. 19

Left large wing:
R1+(last p)3, sp, 1, mp, 1, lp, 3-1.
CH/DK: 1,

Head:
R1+(last p)2, sp, 2-1.
CH/DK: 1,

Right large wing:
R1+(last p)3, lp, 1, mp, 1, sp, 3-1.
CH/DK: 1,

Right small wing:
R1+(last p)2, sp, 1+(first p, R1)2.
CH/DK: 1. End off.
Bring S1's thread through space between base of R1 and first chain knot. Tie a square knot on wrong side of lace.

Neck Chain

~<>—-CTM—-<>~
R5+(head picot of butterfly #2)5.
SR/S1: R5, S2: 5. 41xs.

Butterfly #3 (*Fig. 20*)

Head:
SR/S1: R2-1, S2: 2-1.

Right large wing:
R1+(dk picot of last split ring)3, lp, 1, mp, 1, sp, 3-1.
CH/DK: 1,

Right small wing:
R1+(last p)2, sp, 1-2.
CH/DK:1,

Butt:
R2+(last p)2+(lk, right large wing of Butterfly #1)2-2.
CH/DK: 1,

Left small wing:
R2+(last p)1, sp, 2-1.
CH/DK: 1,

Left large wing:
R1+(last p)3, sp, 1, mp, 1, lp, 3+(head picot)1.
CH/DK: 1. End off.
Bring S1's thread through space between base of last split ring and first chain knot. Tie a square knot on wrong side of lace.

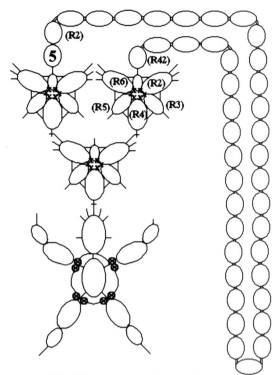

Fig. 20 Completed Chatelaine

Earring or Pin

Using thin thread, work Tatbit motif and Butterfly #1. End off. Bring S1's thread through space between base of last plit ring and first chain knot. Tie a square knot on wrong side of lace. Finish ends. Attach earring wire or pin finding.

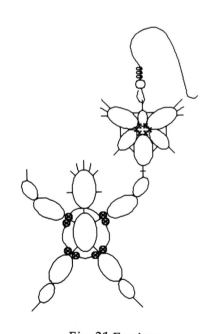

Fig. 21 Earrings